QUICK AND EASY SALAD COOKBOOK

Vibrant And Healthy Salads in Minutes

BLAKE VANOVER

Quick And Easy Salad Cookbook

Introduction

Welcome to the *Quick and Easy Salad Cookbook*! In this book, we'll explore how to make fresh, vibrant salads that are easy to prepare and perfect for any occasion. Whether you're new to salads or a seasoned enthusiast, you'll find something here to inspire your next meal. Each recipe is designed to be quick, easy, and nourishing—ideal for busy days or when you want something light yet satisfying.

Inside, you'll find:

- A guide to creating fresh, flavorful salads in minutes.
- A variety of salads for different occasions, including side salads, meal salads, and more.
- Healthy dressings and toppings that add flavor and texture to your creations.

Salads are not only nutritious, but they can also be exciting and full of flavors. Let's dive into these recipes, and start enjoying fresh salads in no time!

Chapter 1: Fresh & Simple Side Salads

Side salads are the perfect accompaniment to any meal, or they can be enjoyed on their own as a light snack. These quick and easy recipes highlight fresh ingredients and simple dressings that are easy to whip up.

1. Mediterranean Chickpea Salad

- **Prep Time**: 10 minutes
- **Ingredients**:
    - 1 can (15 ounces) chickpeas, drained and rinsed
    - 1 cucumber, diced
    - 1 cup cherry tomatoes, halved
    - 1/4 red onion, thinly sliced
    - 1/4 cup Kalamata olives, pitted
    - 1/4 cup feta cheese, crumbled
    - 2 tablespoons fresh parsley, chopped
    - **Dressing**: 3 tablespoons olive oil, juice of 1 lemon, 1 teaspoon dried oregano, salt and pepper to taste.

- **Instructions**: Combine all salad ingredients in a large bowl. In a small bowl, whisk together the dressing ingredients and pour over the salad. Toss to coat and serve.

2. Simple Avocado and Cucumber Salad

- **Prep Time**: 5 minutes
- **Ingredients**:
    - 1 avocado, diced
    - 1 cucumber, sliced
    - 1 tablespoon olive oil
    - 1 tablespoon fresh lemon juice
    - Salt and pepper to taste
    - Fresh dill for garnish
- **Instructions**: Combine the avocado and cucumber in a bowl. Drizzle with olive oil and lemon juice, then season with salt and pepper. Garnish with dill and serve immediately.

3. Classic Coleslaw

- **Prep Time**: 10 minutes

- **Ingredients**:
    - 4 cups shredded cabbage
    - 1/2 cup grated carrots
    - 1/4 cup red onion, thinly sliced
    - 1/2 cup mayonnaise
    - 1 tablespoon apple cider vinegar
    - 1 tablespoon Dijon mustard
    - Salt and pepper to taste
- **Instructions**: In a large bowl, combine the cabbage, carrots, and red onion. In a separate bowl, whisk together the mayonnaise, vinegar, mustard, salt, and pepper. Pour the dressing over the vegetables and toss to combine.

4. Tomato and Mozzarella Salad

- **Prep Time**: 5 minutes
- **Ingredients**:
    - 2 cups cherry tomatoes, halved
    - 1 cup fresh mozzarella balls, halved
    - Fresh basil leaves, torn

  - 1 tablespoon olive oil
  - 1 tablespoon balsamic vinegar
  - Salt and pepper to taste
- **Instructions**: Combine tomatoes, mozzarella, and basil in a bowl. Drizzle with olive oil and balsamic vinegar, then season with salt and pepper. Toss gently and serve.

5. Carrot and Raisin Salad

- **Prep Time**: 5 minutes
- **Ingredients**:
  - 2 cups shredded carrots
  - 1/4 cup raisins
  - 1/4 cup Greek yogurt
  - 1 tablespoon honey
  - 1 tablespoon lemon juice
- **Instructions**: In a large bowl, combine the carrots and raisins. In a small bowl, whisk together the yogurt, honey, and lemon juice. Pour the dressing over the carrot mixture and toss to coat.

6. Green Bean and Tomato Salad

- **Prep Time**: 10 minutes
- **Ingredients**:
  - 2 cups fresh green beans, blanched
  - 1 cup cherry tomatoes, halved
  - 1/4 cup red onion, thinly sliced
  - 2 tablespoons olive oil
  - 1 tablespoon red wine vinegar
  - Salt and pepper to taste
- **Instructions**: Combine green beans, tomatoes, and onion in a bowl. Whisk together the olive oil, vinegar, salt, and pepper, then drizzle over the salad. Toss to combine.

7. Mixed Greens with Lemon Vinaigrette

- **Prep Time**: 5 minutes
- **Ingredients**:
  - 4 cups mixed greens
  - 1 tablespoon olive oil

  - Juice of 1 lemon
  - Salt and pepper to taste

- **Instructions**: In a bowl, combine the mixed greens. In a small bowl, whisk together olive oil, lemon juice, salt, and pepper. Pour the dressing over the greens and toss to coat.

Chapter 2: Hearty Meal Salads

Meal salads are more substantial and can serve as a complete dish for lunch or dinner. They include a balance of protein, grains, vegetables, and healthy fats, providing a fulfilling and well-rounded meal.

1. Grilled Chicken and Avocado Salad

- **Prep Time**: 10 minutes
- **Cook Time**: 15 minutes
- **Ingredients**:
  - 2 chicken breasts, grilled and sliced
  - 4 cups mixed greens
  - 1 avocado, sliced
  - 1/2 cucumber, sliced
  - 1/4 cup red onion, thinly sliced
  - 1/4 cup feta cheese, crumbled
  - **Dressing**: 3 tablespoons olive oil, juice of 1 lemon, salt and pepper to taste
- **Instructions**: Grill the chicken until fully cooked, then slice thinly. In a bowl, combine the greens,

cucumber, onion, and avocado. Top with sliced chicken and feta. Drizzle with dressing and toss gently.

2. Quinoa and Roasted Vegetable Salad

- **Prep Time**: 15 minutes
- **Cook Time**: 25 minutes
- **Ingredients**:
    - 1 cup quinoa, cooked
    - 2 cups mixed roasted vegetables (e.g., zucchini, bell peppers, carrots)
    - 1/4 cup pumpkin seeds
    - 1/4 cup crumbled feta cheese
    - **Dressing**: 2 tablespoons olive oil, 1 tablespoon balsamic vinegar, salt and pepper to taste
- **Instructions**: Roast vegetables in olive oil at 400°F (200°C) for 20-25 minutes. Combine cooked quinoa and roasted vegetables in a bowl. Drizzle with balsamic dressing, toss, and top with feta and pumpkin seeds.

3. Tuna and Bean Salad

- **Prep Time**: 10 minutes
- **Ingredients**:
    - 1 can tuna, drained
    - 1 can white beans, drained and rinsed
    - 1/2 red onion, thinly sliced
    - 1 cup cherry tomatoes, halved
    - 2 tablespoons olive oil
    - 1 tablespoon lemon juice
- **Instructions**: In a large bowl, combine the tuna, beans, onion, and tomatoes. Drizzle with olive oil and lemon juice, then toss gently.

4. Vegan Buddha Bowl

- **Prep Time**: 15 minutes
- **Cook Time**: 25 minutes
- **Ingredients**:
    - 1 cup cooked quinoa
    - 1 cup roasted sweet potatoes
    - 1/2 cup chickpeas, roasted

    - 1 cup spinach
    - 1/4 avocado, sliced
    - **Dressing**: Tahini, lemon juice, garlic, salt, and pepper

- **Instructions**: Roast sweet potatoes and chickpeas. Layer quinoa, spinach, sweet potatoes, and chickpeas in a bowl. Top with avocado slices and drizzle with tahini dressing.

5. Shrimp and Mango Salad

- **Prep Time**: 10 minutes
- **Cook Time**: 5 minutes
- **Ingredients**:
    - 1/2 pound shrimp, cooked and peeled
    - 1 mango, diced
    - 4 cups mixed greens
    - 1/4 red onion, thinly sliced
    - **Dressing**: 2 tablespoons olive oil, juice of 1 lime, salt and pepper to taste
- **Instructions**: Combine the shrimp, mango, greens, and onion in a bowl. Drizzle with lime

dressing and toss gently.

6. Steak and Roasted Beet Salad

- **Prep Time**: 15 minutes
- **Cook Time**: 10 minutes
- **Ingredients**:
    - 1 steak, grilled and sliced
    - 2 roasted beets, peeled and sliced
    - 4 cups arugula
    - 1/4 cup goat cheese, crumbled
    - **Dressing**: 3 tablespoons olive oil, 1 tablespoon balsamic vinegar, salt and pepper to taste
- **Instructions**: Grill the steak to your desired level, then slice. Combine arugula, roasted beets, and goat cheese. Top with steak slices and drizzle with balsamic vinaigrette.

7. Grilled Chicken Caesar Salad

- **Prep Time**: 10 minutes
- **Cook Time**: 15 minutes

- **Ingredients**:
    - 2 chicken breasts, grilled and sliced
    - 4 cups romaine lettuce
    - 1/4 cup grated Parmesan cheese
    - 1/4 cup croutons
    - **Dressing**: 1/2 cup Caesar dressing
- **Instructions**: Grill the chicken and slice thinly. Toss the romaine with Parmesan, croutons, and Caesar dressing. Top with grilled chicken slices.

Chapter 3: Dressings, Toppings, and Garnishes

Salads are often elevated by the right dressings, toppings, and garnishes. Whether you prefer creamy or tangy dressings, crunchy toppings, or fresh garnishes, this chapter will show you how to add those finishing touches to your salad, bringing both flavor and visual appeal.

1. Classic Vinaigrette

- **Prep Time**: 5 minutes
- **Ingredients**:
  - 1/4 cup extra virgin olive oil
  - 2 tablespoons balsamic vinegar
  - 1 teaspoon Dijon mustard
  - Salt and pepper to taste
- **Instructions**: In a small bowl or jar, whisk together the olive oil, balsamic vinegar, Dijon mustard, salt, and pepper. Drizzle over your salad and toss gently.
- **Tip**: This basic vinaigrette can be customized by adding herbs, garlic, or honey for different flavor profiles.

2. Creamy Avocado Dressing

- **Prep Time**: 5 minutes
- **Ingredients**:
    - 1 ripe avocado
    - 2 tablespoons olive oil
    - 1 tablespoon lime juice
    - 1/4 cup water (more for desired consistency)
    - Salt and pepper to taste
- **Instructions**: In a blender or food processor, combine the avocado, olive oil, lime juice, and water. Blend until smooth, adding more water as needed to reach your desired consistency. Season with salt and pepper.
- **Tip**: For a spicy kick, add a pinch of cayenne pepper or a small jalapeño.

3. Lemon Tahini Dressing

- **Prep Time**: 5 minutes
- **Ingredients**:
    - 3 tablespoons tahini

    - 2 tablespoons lemon juice
    - 1 tablespoon olive oil
    - 1 tablespoon honey (optional)
    - Salt and pepper to taste

- **Instructions**: Whisk together tahini, lemon juice, olive oil, honey (if using), salt, and pepper in a small bowl. Add water to thin out the dressing if necessary.
- **Tip**: This dressing is perfect for Mediterranean or grain-based salads and works well with roasted vegetables.

4. Garlic Parmesan Dressing

- **Prep Time**: 5 minutes
- **Ingredients**:
    - 1/2 cup Greek yogurt
    - 1/4 cup grated Parmesan cheese
    - 1 clove garlic, minced
    - 1 tablespoon lemon juice
    - Salt and pepper to taste

- **Instructions**: In a bowl, combine Greek yogurt, Parmesan cheese, garlic, and lemon juice. Stir until smooth. Season with salt and pepper.
- **Tip**: This dressing is creamy and tangy, making it ideal for Caesar-style salads or any salad that benefits from a cheesy flavor.

5. Cilantro-Lime Dressing

- **Prep Time**: 5 minutes
- **Ingredients**:
  - 1/4 cup fresh cilantro, chopped
  - 3 tablespoons olive oil
  - 2 tablespoons lime juice
  - 1 teaspoon honey (optional)
  - Salt and pepper to taste
- **Instructions**: Whisk together cilantro, olive oil, lime juice, honey (if using), salt, and pepper in a small bowl. Pour over your salad and toss to coat.
- **Tip**: This dressing pairs perfectly with Southwest-style salads or any salad that needs a zesty and herby flavor.

6. Balsamic Glaze

- **Prep Time**: 5 minutes
- **Ingredients**:
    - 1/2 cup balsamic vinegar
    - 1 tablespoon honey or maple syrup
- **Instructions**: In a small saucepan, combine the balsamic vinegar and honey. Bring to a simmer over medium heat, stirring frequently. Cook for 5-7 minutes until the sauce has reduced by half and thickened to a syrupy consistency.
- **Tip**: Drizzle this rich glaze over salads with roasted vegetables or grilled meats to add a sweet and tangy finish.

7. Spicy Sriracha Dressing

- **Prep Time**: 5 minutes
- **Ingredients**:
    - 1/4 cup mayonnaise
    - 2 tablespoons sriracha sauce
    - 1 tablespoon lime juice
    - 1 teaspoon honey

- **Instructions**: In a bowl, combine mayonnaise, sriracha, lime juice, and honey. Stir until smooth and well combined.

- **Tip**: This spicy dressing adds a bold kick to salads and works particularly well with Asian-inspired salads or noodle bowls.

Toppings: Adding Crunch, Richness, and Flavor

Toppings are essential to making salads exciting and filling. From nuts and seeds to cheeses and roasted vegetables, toppings add texture, flavor, and nutritional value to any salad.

1. Toasted Almonds

- **Prep Time**: 5 minutes

- **Ingredients**:

    - 1/2 cup sliced almonds

- **Instructions**: Toast the almonds in a dry skillet over medium heat for 5-7 minutes, stirring frequently until golden and fragrant.

- **Tip**: Toasted almonds add a nutty crunch to salads and pair especially well with leafy greens, berries, and citrus-based dressings.

2. Crispy Chickpeas

- **Prep Time**: 10 minutes
- **Cook Time**: 25 minutes
- **Ingredients**:
    - 1 can (15 ounces) chickpeas, drained and rinsed
    - 1 tablespoon olive oil
    - 1 teaspoon paprika
    - Salt to taste
- **Instructions**: Preheat the oven to 400°F (200°C). Toss the chickpeas with olive oil, paprika, and salt. Spread on a baking sheet and roast for 20-25 minutes until crispy.
- **Tip**: These crispy chickpeas are a great plant-based topping for any salad and offer a crunchy, protein-packed addition.

3. Crumbled Feta Cheese

- **Prep Time**: 1 minute
- **Ingredients**:
    - 1/4 cup feta cheese, crumbled

- **Instructions**: Simply crumble feta cheese over the salad.
- **Tip**: Feta adds a creamy, tangy flavor that works well with Mediterranean-inspired salads and roasted vegetables.

4. Roasted Pumpkin Seeds

- **Prep Time**: 5 minutes
- **Cook Time**: 10 minutes
- **Ingredients**:
    - 1/2 cup raw pumpkin seeds
    - 1 tablespoon olive oil
    - 1 teaspoon chili powder
- **Instructions**: Preheat the oven to 375°F (190°C). Toss the pumpkin seeds with olive oil and chili powder. Roast for 10 minutes, stirring once, until crispy.
- **Tip**: Pumpkin seeds add a crunchy, slightly spicy topping to any salad, especially those with roasted vegetables or a Mexican-inspired flavor.

5. Sunflower Seeds

- **Prep Time**: 2 minutes
- **Ingredients**:
  - 1/4 cup sunflower seeds
- **Instructions**: Sprinkle sunflower seeds over your salad for an extra crunch and nutty flavor.
- **Tip**: Sunflower seeds are great for adding texture and are a good source of healthy fats and vitamin E.

6. Shaved Parmesan

- **Prep Time**: 1 minute
- **Ingredients**:
  - 1/4 cup Parmesan cheese, shaved
- **Instructions**: Use a vegetable peeler to shave Parmesan cheese directly over your salad.
- **Tip**: Shaved Parmesan adds richness and depth to any salad and pairs particularly well with Caesar or Italian-style salads.

7. Crispy Fried Shallots

- **Prep Time**: 5 minutes

- **Cook Time**: 10 minutes
- **Ingredients**:
  - 2 shallots, thinly sliced
  - 1/2 cup flour
  - Salt to taste
- **Instructions**: Heat oil in a skillet over medium heat. Dredge the shallots in flour and fry for 5-7 minutes until golden and crispy. Drain on paper towels.
- **Tip**: Crispy fried shallots add a savory, crunchy topping to salads, especially those with Asian or French-inspired flavors.

Garnishes: Elevating the Salad's Appearance and Taste

Garnishes are the final flourish that can make your salad look and taste more vibrant and exciting. Here are some ideas to help you garnish your salads beautifully.

1. Fresh Herbs

- **How to Use**: Fresh herbs like parsley, cilantro, basil, or mint can be chopped and sprinkled over salads for added flavor and freshness.

- **Tip**: Fresh herbs are best added at the end to preserve their color and delicate flavor.

2. Edible Flowers

- **How to Use**: Garnish your salad with edible flowers such as pansies, marigolds, or nasturtiums. These flowers add a pop of color and a delicate flavor.
- **Tip**: Use sparingly to avoid overwhelming the salad, and make sure the flowers are pesticide-free.

3. Lemon Zest

- **How to Use**: Use a zester or microplane to grate fresh lemon zest over your salad for a burst of citrusy aroma.
- **Tip**: Lemon zest is a perfect garnish for salads with avocado, grilled chicken, or seafood.

4. Pomegranate Seeds

- **How to Use**: Sprinkle pomegranate seeds over your salad for a burst of sweetness and color.
- **Tip**: Pomegranate seeds are especially beautiful in salads with greens, nuts, or grains.

Chapter 4: Building the Perfect Salad Bowl

A well-balanced salad bowl is the perfect meal in a bowl, providing a delicious mix of textures, flavors, and nutritional benefits. In this chapter, we'll explore how to build the perfect salad bowl from the ground up, using a variety of base ingredients, proteins, vegetables, toppings, and dressings. Whether you're craving a hearty meal salad or a lighter, refreshing option, we'll guide you through the process of creating a customized salad that is both satisfying and healthy.

The Salad Bowl Formula: Layering Ingredients for Balance

A well-designed salad bowl should have a balance of protein, healthy fats, fiber, and carbs to make it a fulfilling and complete meal. Here's a simple formula for creating the perfect salad bowl:

1. **Start with a Base**: This can be greens or grains, or even a combination of both.

2. **Add Protein**: Include a source of protein to keep you full longer—this could be meat, seafood, tofu, or legumes.

3. **Add Veggies**: Incorporate a variety of vegetables for different textures and a wide array of vitamins and minerals.

4. **Include Healthy Fats**: Fats from avocado, nuts, seeds, or cheese help provide satiety and flavor.

5. **Top with Crunch**: Add crunch with nuts, seeds, or crispy roasted vegetables to keep the salad interesting.

6. **Drizzle with Dressing**: Choose a dressing that complements the other ingredients, bringing the salad together.

Let's explore a few salad bowl ideas, breaking down the ingredients so you can create your own customizable options!

1. Grilled Chicken Salad Bowl

- **Base**: Mixed greens (spinach, arugula, or lettuce)
- **Protein**: Grilled chicken breast, sliced
- **Veggies**: Cherry tomatoes, cucumber, red onion, roasted sweet potato cubes
- **Healthy Fats**: Sliced avocado
- **Crunch**: Pumpkin seeds
- **Dressing**: Lemon-balsamic vinaigrette

Instructions: Start with a bed of mixed greens. Layer on the grilled chicken, followed by the veggies and roasted sweet potatoes. Top with avocado and pumpkin seeds for crunch. Drizzle with a fresh lemon-balsamic vinaigrette and toss gently.

Nutritional Benefits: This salad is a protein-packed powerhouse, providing lean chicken and healthy fats from avocado, while the veggies contribute essential vitamins and fiber.

2. Vegan Buddha Bowl

- **Base**: Quinoa or brown rice
- **Protein**: Roasted chickpeas
- **Veggies**: Roasted cauliflower, steamed broccoli, shredded carrots, and cucumber
- **Healthy Fats**: Sliced avocado
- **Crunch**: Toasted sunflower seeds
- **Dressing**: Tahini-lemon dressing

Instructions: Layer quinoa or brown rice at the bottom of the bowl. Add roasted chickpeas and vegetables. Top with avocado slices, toasted sunflower seeds, and drizzle with tahini-lemon dressing. Toss and enjoy!

Nutritional Benefits: This bowl offers a balanced mix of complex carbs, plant-based protein, fiber, and healthy fats, making it an ideal vegan meal.

3. Tuna Poke Bowl

- **Base**: Jasmine rice or sushi rice
- **Protein**: Fresh tuna, cubed
- **Veggies**: Sliced cucumber, shredded carrots, edamame, seaweed salad
- **Healthy Fats**: Sliced avocado
- **Crunch**: Crispy fried onions
- **Dressing**: Soy sauce, sesame oil, and rice vinegar

Instructions: Start with a layer of rice, then top with fresh tuna, cucumber, carrots, edamame, and seaweed salad. Add slices of avocado and a sprinkle of crispy fried onions. Drizzle with a soy-sesame dressing and mix gently.

Nutritional Benefits: High in protein from tuna and edamame, healthy fats from avocado, and packed with nutrients from the vegetables and sesame oil dressing.

4. Mexican-Inspired Salad Bowl

- **Base**: Romaine lettuce or mixed greens
- **Protein**: Grilled chicken or black beans (for a vegetarian version)
- **Veggies**: Corn, cherry tomatoes, red onion, bell peppers, jalapeño
- **Healthy Fats**: Guacamole or sliced avocado
- **Crunch**: Tortilla strips or crushed tortilla chips
- **Dressing**: Lime-cilantro dressing

Instructions: Start with romaine lettuce or mixed greens, then layer on the grilled chicken or black beans. Add your choice of veggies and top with guacamole or avocado slices. Garnish with crunchy tortilla strips and drizzle with a zesty lime-cilantro dressing.

Nutritional Benefits: This salad is rich in protein and fiber, with the healthy fats from avocado and guacamole keeping you satisfied.

5. Mediterranean Salad Bowl

- **Base**: Mixed greens (spinach, arugula, and lettuce)

- **Protein**: Grilled chicken or falafel
- **Veggies**: Cucumber, cherry tomatoes, red onion, Kalamata olives
- **Healthy Fats**: Feta cheese or hummus
- **Crunch**: Toasted pine nuts
- **Dressing**: Lemon-oregano vinaigrette

Instructions: Layer mixed greens at the base of the bowl, then add grilled chicken or falafel, followed by fresh veggies and olives. Top with crumbled feta or a scoop of hummus, toasted pine nuts, and drizzle with lemon-oregano vinaigrette.

Nutritional Benefits: This Mediterranean-inspired bowl offers protein from chicken or falafel, healthy fats from feta and olives, and fiber from the veggies, making it a well-rounded meal.

6. Smoked Salmon and Avocado Salad Bowl

- **Base**: Arugula or mixed greens
- **Protein**: Smoked salmon
- **Veggies**: Cucumber, cherry tomatoes, red onion

- **Healthy Fats**: Sliced avocado
- **Crunch**: Pumpkin seeds or sesame seeds
- **Dressing**: Dill yogurt dressing

Instructions: Start with a base of greens, then layer with smoked salmon, cucumber, tomatoes, and red onion. Top with sliced avocado and crunchy seeds. Drizzle with dill yogurt dressing for a creamy, tangy finish.

Nutritional Benefits: This bowl provides heart-healthy omega-3s from smoked salmon, healthy fats from avocado, and antioxidants from the vegetables.

7. Cobb Salad Bowl

- **Base**: Romaine lettuce or mixed greens
- **Protein**: Grilled chicken, hard-boiled eggs, and bacon
- **Veggies**: Cherry tomatoes, avocado, cucumber, and red onion
- **Healthy Fats**: Blue cheese
- **Crunch**: Croutons

- **Dressing**: Ranch dressing or blue cheese dressing

Instructions: Layer romaine lettuce with grilled chicken, sliced hard-boiled eggs, and crispy bacon. Add fresh veggies and top with avocado, blue cheese, and croutons. Drizzle with your favorite dressing and serve.

Nutritional Benefits: This hearty salad provides a good mix of protein from chicken and eggs, healthy fats from avocado and blue cheese, and fiber from the veggies.

Salad Bowl Tips

- **Base Choices**: Use a variety of greens or grains like quinoa, brown rice, farro, or couscous for a more filling meal.

- **Protein Ideas**: If you're vegetarian, use plant-based proteins like chickpeas, tofu, or tempeh. For meat lovers, try grilled chicken, steak, shrimp, or salmon.

- **Mix It Up**: Experiment with different vegetables to keep your salads fresh and exciting. Roasted vegetables like sweet potatoes or cauliflower add a delicious twist.

- **Dressing Variations**: Don't be afraid to mix and match dressings! A simple vinaigrette pairs well with almost any salad, while creamy dressings like ranch or Caesar can make your salad extra indulgent.

- **Garnishes and Toppings**: Get creative with your toppings—try adding roasted chickpeas, fried onions, or toasted nuts for added flavor and texture.

Chapter 5: Meal Prep Salads: Prepare Ahead for Convenience

One of the best ways to ensure that you're eating healthy, satisfying meals throughout the week is to prep your salads in advance. Meal prep salads allow you to enjoy fresh, vibrant meals without spending hours in the kitchen every day. This chapter will show you how to prep your salads ahead of time while maintaining their freshness and flavor. We'll explore tips for storing ingredients, assembling salads for the week, and ways to keep your salads crispy and delicious.

The Basics of Meal Prep Salads

Meal prepping doesn't have to be complicated. The goal is to prep your ingredients, store them properly, and assemble the salads quickly when you're ready to eat. Here's the step-by-step guide:

1. **Choose Salad Bases**: Select hearty greens that can handle being stored for several days without wilting. Some great options include romaine lettuce, kale, spinach, or arugula. You can also use grains like quinoa, farro, or brown rice as a base for a more filling salad.

2. **Store Ingredients Separately**: Keep dressing, protein, and vegetables in separate containers to avoid sogginess. Store wet ingredients like tomatoes, cucumbers, and avocado in

containers that allow them to breathe.

3. **Layering for Freshness**: If you plan to store your salads in jars (like mason jars), use the "wet on the bottom, dry on top" method. Start with dressing at the bottom, followed by hearty ingredients like beans, grains, or proteins, and end with greens at the top.

4. **Keep the Dressing Separate**: Dressings should always be stored separately and added right before serving to prevent the salad from becoming soggy.

5. **Pack in Airtight Containers**: Use airtight containers or mason jars to keep the salads fresh for up to 4 days. This ensures your ingredients stay crisp and vibrant.

1. Chicken and Quinoa Salad for the Week

This salad is high in protein and fiber, making it a filling and nutritious option for meal prep. It stays fresh for up to 4 days when stored correctly.

- **Prep Time**: 20 minutes
- **Ingredients**:

1. 2 chicken breasts, grilled and sliced
2. 1 cup quinoa, cooked
3. 1 cup cherry tomatoes, halved
4. 1 cucumber, sliced
5. 1/4 cup red onion, thinly sliced
6. 1/4 cup feta cheese, crumbled
7. **Dressing**: 2 tablespoons olive oil, 1 tablespoon lemon juice, 1 teaspoon Dijon mustard, salt and pepper to taste

- **Instructions**:

1. Cook quinoa according to package instructions. Let it cool.
2. Grill chicken breasts and slice them thinly.
3. Combine the quinoa, chicken, cherry tomatoes, cucumber, red onion, and feta in separate containers or jars.
4. Store dressing in a small jar or container to keep it separate from the salad.
5. When ready to eat, drizzle the dressing over the salad and toss.

- **Storage Tips**: Store the salad components in an airtight container in the fridge. Add the dressing just before serving to keep everything fresh.

2. Tuna Salad Bowl

This tuna salad is a great option for meal prepping, and it stays fresh for up to 3 days. It's high in protein and healthy fats, making it an excellent choice for a balanced meal.

- **Prep Time**: 15 minutes
- **Ingredients**:
    1. 1 can tuna, drained
    2. 1/2 cup chickpeas, rinsed
    3. 1 cup mixed greens
    4. 1/2 cucumber, diced
    5. 1/4 cup Kalamata olives, pitted
    6. 1/4 cup red onion, thinly sliced
    7. **Dressing**: 3 tablespoons olive oil, 1 tablespoon lemon juice, 1 teaspoon dried oregano, salt and pepper to taste

- **Instructions**:

    1. Drain the tuna and place it in a large bowl.
    2. Add the chickpeas, mixed greens, cucumber, olives, and red onion to the bowl.
    3. Store in an airtight container with the dressing on the side.
    4. When ready to eat, pour the dressing over the salad and toss gently.

- **Storage Tips**: Store the salad and the dressing separately in airtight containers. This will keep the greens fresh and prevent wilting.

3. Vegan Roasted Vegetable and Chickpea Salad

This vegan salad is packed with flavor and nutrients, making it an ideal option for a filling meal prep. The roasted vegetables add depth, and the chickpeas provide protein.

- **Prep Time**: 25 minutes
- **Ingredients**:

1. 1 can chickpeas, drained and rinsed
2. 2 cups mixed vegetables (zucchini, bell peppers, carrots), chopped
3. 1 tablespoon olive oil
4. Salt and pepper to taste
5. 1/2 cup quinoa, cooked
6. 2 cups spinach
7. **Dressing**: 2 tablespoons tahini, 1 tablespoon lemon juice, 1 teaspoon maple syrup, water to thin

- **Instructions**:

1. Preheat the oven to 400°F (200°C). Toss the chopped vegetables with olive oil, salt, and pepper. Roast in the oven for 20-25 minutes until tender.
2. Cook quinoa according to package instructions and let it cool.
3. In a large bowl, combine the roasted vegetables, chickpeas, quinoa, and spinach.
4. Store in airtight containers with the dressing on the side.

5. When ready to eat, drizzle the tahini dressing over the salad and toss.

- **Storage Tips**: This salad stays fresh in the fridge for up to 4 days when stored properly. Keep the dressing separate to preserve the texture of the vegetables.

4. Grilled Steak Salad with Roasted Sweet Potatoes

A hearty salad with tender steak, roasted sweet potatoes, and crunchy greens. Perfect for meal prepping and full of satisfying flavors.

- **Prep Time**: 15 minutes
- **Cook Time**: 25 minutes
- **Ingredients**:
  1. 2 steak fillets, grilled and sliced
  2. 2 sweet potatoes, cubed and roasted
  3. 2 cups arugula or mixed greens
  4. 1/4 cup crumbled blue cheese
  5. **Dressing**: 2 tablespoons olive oil, 1 tablespoon balsamic vinegar, 1 teaspoon

Dijon mustard, salt and pepper to taste

- **Instructions**:

    1. Grill the steaks to your desired level and slice thinly.
    2. Roast the sweet potato cubes with olive oil, salt, and pepper at 400°F (200°C) for 20-25 minutes until tender.
    3. In an airtight container, layer the greens, roasted sweet potatoes, grilled steak slices, and blue cheese.
    4. Store the dressing separately in a small container.
    5. When ready to eat, drizzle the dressing over the salad and toss.

- **Storage Tips**: The steak and sweet potatoes can be stored separately in airtight containers for up to 4 days. Keep the dressing in a separate container to avoid sogginess.

5. Mediterranean Falafel Salad

This salad is loaded with Mediterranean flavors, with crispy falafel, fresh vegetables, and a tangy dressing. It's perfect for meal prep and stays fresh for 3-4 days.

- **Prep Time**: 20 minutes
- **Cook Time**: 20 minutes
- **Ingredients**:
  1. 1 batch of homemade or store-bought falafel
  2. 1 cup mixed greens
  3. 1/4 cup cherry tomatoes, halved
  4. 1/4 cucumber, sliced
  5. 1/4 cup red onion, thinly sliced
  6. 2 tablespoons Kalamata olives, pitted
  7. **Dressing**: 3 tablespoons tahini, 1 tablespoon lemon juice, 1 teaspoon olive oil, water to thin, salt and pepper to taste
- **Instructions**:
  1. Cook the falafel according to package instructions or make your own.
  2. In an airtight container, layer the mixed greens, tomatoes, cucumber, red onion, and olives.
  3. Store the falafel separately and add them just before serving.

4. For the dressing, whisk together tahini, lemon juice, olive oil, and water. Drizzle over the salad when ready to eat.

- **Storage Tips**: Keep the falafel separate until you're ready to eat to maintain their crispiness. Store the dressing separately as well.

6. Asian-Inspired Tofu Salad

A plant-based salad full of flavors from sesame oil, ginger, and tofu. This meal prep-friendly salad is great for vegan or vegetarian diets.

- **Prep Time**: 10 minutes
- **Cook Time**: 15 minutes
- **Ingredients**:

1. 1 block tofu, pressed and cubed
2. 2 cups mixed greens (spinach, arugula, or kale)
3. 1/2 cucumber, julienned
4. 1/4 cup shredded carrots
5. 1/4 cup edamame, shelled

6. **Dressing**: 2 tablespoons soy sauce, 1 tablespoon sesame oil, 1 teaspoon rice vinegar, 1 teaspoon grated ginger, 1 teaspoon honey (optional)

- **Instructions**:

  1. Pan-fry or bake the tofu cubes until crispy.
  2. In a bowl, combine the mixed greens, cucumber, carrots, and edamame.
  3. Store the tofu and dressing separately from the salad in airtight containers.
  4. When ready to eat, top the salad with tofu and drizzle with the sesame-soy dressing.

- **Storage Tips**: Store the tofu and dressing separately to preserve the texture of both. This salad stays fresh for 3-4 days in the fridge.

7. Caprese Salad with Grilled Chicken

A simple yet satisfying salad with grilled chicken, fresh tomatoes, mozzarella, and basil. This is perfect for meal prepping when you're craving something light but filling.

- **Prep Time**: 10 minutes
- **Cook Time**: 10 minutes
- **Ingredients**:
    1. 2 grilled chicken breasts, sliced
    2. 2 cups arugula or mixed greens
    3. 1 cup cherry tomatoes, halved
    4. 1/4 cup fresh mozzarella balls, halved
    5. Fresh basil leaves
    6. **Dressing**: 2 tablespoons balsamic vinegar, 2 tablespoons olive oil, salt and pepper to taste
- **Instructions**:
    1. Grill the chicken breasts until fully cooked and slice.
    2. In a bowl, combine the greens, tomatoes, mozzarella, and basil.
    3. Store the chicken separately and add it just before serving.
    4. Drizzle the balsamic dressing over the salad and toss.

- **Storage Tips**: This salad can be prepped for 3-4 days, with the chicken stored separately to maintain its freshness.

Chapter 6: Seasonal Salads: Embracing Fresh, Seasonal Ingredients

One of the joys of salad-making is the opportunity to use fresh, seasonal ingredients that are at their peak. Seasonal salads allow you to explore the full range of flavors each season has to offer, from crisp spring greens to hearty fall squash. In this chapter, we'll dive into how to build salads around the seasons, making the most of what's available at any time of year. By focusing on seasonal ingredients, you'll not only get the best flavor but also ensure your salads are packed with nutrients.

Why Seasonal Ingredients?

Seasonal ingredients are grown at the time when they're meant to thrive, so they tend to be fresher, tastier, and more affordable. Eating with the seasons also allows you to support local farmers, reduce your carbon footprint, and enjoy a variety of flavors throughout the year. Each season brings a new bounty of vegetables, fruits, and herbs, and with them comes the perfect opportunity to create vibrant salads.

Spring Salads: Light, Crisp, and Fresh

Spring is all about fresh, tender greens, vibrant herbs, and early-season vegetables like asparagus, peas, and radishes. These ingredients are perfect for light, refreshing salads that celebrate the changing weather.

1. Spring Greens and Pea Salad

- **Prep Time**: 10 minutes
- **Ingredients**:
    1. 2 cups mixed spring greens (arugula, spinach, and baby kale)
    2. 1/2 cup fresh peas (or frozen peas, thawed)
    3. 1/4 cup radishes, thinly sliced
    4. 1/4 cup goat cheese, crumbled
    5. **Dressing**: 2 tablespoons olive oil, 1 tablespoon lemon juice, 1 teaspoon honey, salt and pepper to taste
- **Instructions**:
    1. Combine the spring greens, peas, and radishes in a bowl.

2. Top with crumbled goat cheese.
3. Whisk together the olive oil, lemon juice, honey, salt, and pepper in a small bowl and drizzle over the salad. Toss gently and serve.

- **Nutritional Benefits**: Spring greens are high in vitamins A and C, while peas provide protein and fiber. Goat cheese adds calcium and a creamy texture.

2. Asparagus and Strawberry Salad

- **Prep Time**: 10 minutes
- **Ingredients**:

1. 1 bunch asparagus, trimmed and blanched
2. 1 cup strawberries, sliced
3. 2 cups arugula
4. 1/4 cup toasted almonds
5. **Dressing**: 2 tablespoons balsamic vinegar, 1 tablespoon olive oil, 1 teaspoon maple syrup, salt and pepper to taste

- **Instructions**:

    1. Blanch the asparagus by boiling it for 2-3 minutes, then immediately transferring it to ice water to stop the cooking process.

    2. Combine the asparagus, strawberries, and arugula in a bowl.

    3. Drizzle with balsamic vinegar dressing and top with toasted almonds. Toss and serve.

- **Nutritional Benefits**: Asparagus is rich in vitamins K and C, while strawberries provide antioxidants and vitamin C. Almonds add healthy fats and crunch.

3. Baby Carrot and Radish Salad

- **Prep Time**: 8 minutes

- **Ingredients**:

    1. 1 cup baby carrots, sliced into thin coins

    2. 1/2 cup radishes, sliced

    3. 1 tablespoon fresh parsley, chopped

    4. 1/4 cup crumbled feta cheese

5. **Dressing**: 3 tablespoons olive oil, 1 tablespoon apple cider vinegar, 1 teaspoon Dijon mustard, salt and pepper to taste

- **Instructions**:

1. Combine the carrots, radishes, and parsley in a bowl.
2. Add crumbled feta cheese on top.
3. Whisk together the dressing ingredients and pour over the salad. Toss and enjoy!

- **Nutritional Benefits**: Carrots are full of beta-carotene and fiber, while radishes are low in calories but rich in vitamin C. Feta cheese adds a creamy, tangy kick.

Summer Salads: Bright, Juicy, and Refreshing

Summer brings a bounty of juicy fruits and vegetables, perfect for cooling off and enjoying the vibrant flavors of the season. Think tomatoes, cucumbers, peaches, and berries, all of which make excellent salad ingredients.

4. Watermelon, Cucumber, and Mint Salad

- **Prep Time**: 5 minutes
- **Ingredients**:
    1. 2 cups watermelon, cubed
    2. 1 cucumber, diced
    3. 1/4 cup fresh mint leaves, chopped
    4. 1/4 cup feta cheese, crumbled
    5. **Dressing**: 1 tablespoon olive oil, 1 tablespoon lime juice, salt and pepper to taste
- **Instructions**:
    1. Combine the watermelon, cucumber, and mint in a bowl.
    2. Top with crumbled feta cheese.
    3. Drizzle with olive oil and lime dressing and toss to combine. Serve chilled.
- **Nutritional Benefits**: Watermelon is hydrating and rich in antioxidants, while cucumbers are low in calories and high in water content. Feta adds a savory, creamy element.

5. Peach and Burrata Salad

- **Prep Time**: 10 minutes
- **Ingredients**:
    1. 2 ripe peaches, sliced
    2. 1 ball burrata cheese
    3. 2 cups arugula
    4. 1/4 cup pistachios, crushed
    5. **Dressing**: 1 tablespoon honey, 2 tablespoons olive oil, 1 tablespoon lemon juice, salt and pepper to taste
- **Instructions**:
    1. Arrange the peach slices, arugula, and burrata on a serving platter.
    2. Drizzle with honey, olive oil, and lemon juice dressing.
    3. Top with crushed pistachios for crunch.
- **Nutritional Benefits**: Peaches are a great source of vitamin C and fiber, while burrata adds protein and creaminess. Pistachios provide healthy fats and extra crunch.

6. Tomato and Corn Salad

- **Prep Time**: 10 minutes
- **Ingredients**:
    1. 1 pint cherry tomatoes, halved
    2. 1 cup corn kernels (fresh or frozen)
    3. 1/4 red onion, thinly sliced
    4. 1 tablespoon cilantro, chopped
    5. **Dressing**: 2 tablespoons olive oil, 1 tablespoon lime juice, 1 teaspoon chili powder, salt and pepper to taste
- **Instructions**:
    1. Combine tomatoes, corn, and red onion in a bowl.
    2. Drizzle with olive oil, lime juice, and chili powder dressing.
    3. Garnish with fresh cilantro and toss to combine.
- **Nutritional Benefits**: This salad is full of vitamin C from the tomatoes and lime juice, and fiber from the corn. It's also a good source of antioxidants.

Fall Salads: Warm, Hearty, and Comforting

Fall is the season for root vegetables, squashes, and hearty greens. These ingredients make for filling and satisfying salads, perfect for cooler weather.

7. Roasted Butternut Squash and Kale Salad

- **Prep Time**: 10 minutes
- **Cook Time**: 30 minutes
- **Ingredients**:
    1. 2 cups butternut squash, peeled and cubed
    2. 2 cups kale, chopped
    3. 1/4 cup pomegranate seeds
    4. 1/4 cup toasted walnuts
    5. **Dressing**: 2 tablespoons olive oil, 1 tablespoon maple syrup, 1 tablespoon apple cider vinegar, salt and pepper to taste
- **Instructions**:
    1. Preheat the oven to 400°F (200°C). Roast the squash with olive oil, salt, and

pepper for 25-30 minutes, or until tender.

2. Massage the kale with a little olive oil to soften it.
3. Combine the roasted squash, kale, pomegranate seeds, and walnuts in a bowl.
4. Drizzle with maple syrup dressing and toss gently.

- **Nutritional Benefits**: Butternut squash is high in vitamins A and C, while kale provides fiber and antioxidants. Walnuts offer healthy fats and omega-3s.

8. Apple and Spinach Salad with Walnuts

- **Prep Time**: 5 minutes
- **Ingredients**:

1. 2 cups spinach, chopped
2. 1 apple, thinly sliced
3. 1/4 cup walnuts, toasted
4. 1/4 cup blue cheese, crumbled

5. **Dressing**: 2 tablespoons balsamic vinegar, 1 tablespoon olive oil, 1 teaspoon honey, salt and pepper to taste

- **Instructions**:

  1. Combine spinach, apple slices, and blue cheese in a bowl.

  2. Top with toasted walnuts.

  3. Drizzle with balsamic dressing and toss gently.

- **Nutritional Benefits**: Apples provide fiber and vitamin C, while spinach adds vitamins A and K. Walnuts contribute healthy fats and a satisfying crunch.

Chapter 7: Customizing Salads for Your Dietary Needs

Salads can be tailored to meet various dietary preferences, restrictions, and health goals. Whether you're following a specific diet like keto, gluten-free, paleo, or vegan, or if you're simply trying to make healthier choices, there's a salad recipe out there for you. In this chapter, we will explore how to modify and customize your salads to suit a variety of dietary needs while still keeping them delicious, balanced, and satisfying.

1. Keto-Friendly Salads: Low-Carb, High-Fat

The keto diet emphasizes a high intake of healthy fats, moderate protein, and minimal carbohydrates. When creating keto-friendly salads, focus on leafy greens, healthy fats, and protein-rich ingredients, while avoiding high-carb vegetables like potatoes and corn.

Keto Cobb Salad

- **Prep Time**: 10 minutes
- **Ingredients**:
    1. 2 cups romaine lettuce
    2. 2 hard-boiled eggs, chopped

3. 1/2 avocado, sliced
4. 1/4 cup crumbled blue cheese
5. 1/2 grilled chicken breast, sliced
6. 1/4 cup crispy bacon, crumbled
7. **Dressing**: 2 tablespoons olive oil, 1 tablespoon apple cider vinegar, 1 teaspoon Dijon mustard, salt, and pepper to taste

- **Instructions**:

1. In a large bowl, combine the romaine lettuce, eggs, avocado, blue cheese, chicken, and bacon.
2. In a small bowl, whisk together the olive oil, apple cider vinegar, Dijon mustard, salt, and pepper.
3. Drizzle the dressing over the salad and toss gently.

- **Nutritional Benefits**: This salad is rich in protein from the chicken and eggs, healthy fats from avocado and olive oil, and fiber from the leafy greens.

2. Gluten-Free Salads: Safe and Satisfying

For those avoiding gluten, the key to a gluten-free salad is using ingredients that are naturally gluten-free, like fresh fruits, vegetables, nuts, seeds, and gluten-free grains like quinoa or rice. Avoid packaged dressings or toppings that may contain gluten.

Quinoa and Roasted Vegetable Salad (Gluten-Free)

- **Prep Time**: 10 minutes
- **Cook Time**: 25 minutes
- **Ingredients**:
    1. 1 cup quinoa, cooked
    2. 2 cups mixed roasted vegetables (zucchini, bell peppers, onions)
    3. 2 tablespoons olive oil
    4. 1/4 cup fresh basil, chopped
    5. 1/4 cup feta cheese (optional)
    6. **Dressing**: 2 tablespoons olive oil, 1 tablespoon balsamic vinegar, 1 teaspoon honey, salt, and pepper
- **Instructions**:
    1. Preheat the oven to 400°F (200°C). Toss the vegetables with olive oil and season with salt and pepper. Roast for 20-25

minutes until tender.

2. Combine the cooked quinoa, roasted vegetables, and fresh basil in a bowl.
3. Drizzle with balsamic dressing and toss gently. Top with feta cheese if desired.

- **Nutritional Benefits**: Quinoa is a great gluten-free source of protein and fiber. The roasted vegetables add vitamins and antioxidants, while olive oil and feta provide healthy fats.

3. Paleo Salads: Whole, Unprocessed Ingredients

The paleo diet focuses on whole, unprocessed foods such as lean meats, fish, fruits, vegetables, nuts, and seeds. Paleo-friendly salads are packed with fresh, natural ingredients and avoid grains, legumes, and dairy.

Paleo Grilled Chicken Salad

- **Prep Time**: 10 minutes
- **Cook Time**: 15 minutes
- **Ingredients**:

1. 2 grilled chicken breasts, sliced

2. 2 cups mixed greens (spinach, arugula, and kale)
3. 1/4 cucumber, sliced
4. 1/4 cup sliced almonds
5. 1/4 cup pomegranate seeds
6. **Dressing**: 2 tablespoons olive oil, 1 tablespoon lemon juice, 1 teaspoon Dijon mustard, salt, and pepper

- **Instructions**:
  1. Grill the chicken breasts until fully cooked and slice them thinly.
  2. In a bowl, combine the mixed greens, cucumber, sliced almonds, and pomegranate seeds.
  3. Drizzle with olive oil, lemon juice, and Dijon mustard dressing. Toss to combine.
- **Nutritional Benefits**: This salad provides protein from the chicken, healthy fats from olive oil and almonds, and antioxidants from the pomegranate.

4. Vegan Salads: Plant-Based Goodness

Vegan salads are made entirely from plant-based ingredients, offering a wealth of fiber, antioxidants, and healthy fats. These salads typically include grains, legumes, nuts, seeds, and lots of colorful vegetables.

Vegan Chickpea Salad

- **Prep Time**: 10 minutes
- **Ingredients**:
    1. 1 can chickpeas, drained and rinsed
    2. 2 cups spinach
    3. 1/2 cucumber, diced
    4. 1/4 red onion, thinly sliced
    5. 1/4 cup avocado, diced
    6. 1 tablespoon sesame seeds
    7. **Dressing**: 2 tablespoons tahini, 1 tablespoon lemon juice, 1 teaspoon maple syrup, water to thin
- **Instructions**:
    1. Combine the chickpeas, spinach, cucumber, red onion, and avocado in a bowl.
    2. In a small bowl, whisk together tahini, lemon juice, maple syrup, and water until

smooth.

3. Drizzle the dressing over the salad and sprinkle with sesame seeds. Toss gently.

- **Nutritional Benefits**: Chickpeas provide plant-based protein and fiber, while avocado adds healthy fats. The tahini dressing offers additional richness and flavor.

5. Low-Sodium Salads: Flavor Without the Salt

For individuals who are watching their sodium intake, it's important to create salads with low-sodium ingredients. Fresh fruits, vegetables, and homemade dressings are perfect for keeping sodium levels low while still delivering great flavor.

Low-Sodium Kale and Apple Salad

- **Prep Time**: 10 minutes
- **Ingredients**:
  1. 2 cups kale, chopped
  2. 1 apple, sliced
  3. 1/4 cup walnuts, toasted

4. 1 tablespoon chia seeds
5. **Dressing**: 2 tablespoons olive oil, 1 tablespoon apple cider vinegar, 1 teaspoon honey, black pepper to taste

- **Instructions**:
  1. Massage the kale with olive oil to soften it.
  2. Add the apple slices, walnuts, and chia seeds to the kale.
  3. In a small bowl, whisk together the dressing ingredients and pour over the salad. Toss gently.
- **Nutritional Benefits**: Kale provides fiber and antioxidants, while walnuts offer healthy fats. The apple adds sweetness without the need for added sodium.

6. Low-Calorie Salads: Light and Nourishing

Low-calorie salads are great for those looking to reduce calorie intake while still enjoying a satisfying meal. Focus on fresh vegetables, lean proteins, and light dressings to keep the calorie count low.

Light Shrimp Salad

- **Prep Time**: 10 minutes
- **Cook Time**: 5 minutes
- **Ingredients**:
    1. 1/2 pound shrimp, cooked and peeled
    2. 2 cups mixed greens (spinach, arugula, lettuce)
    3. 1/4 cup cucumber, sliced
    4. 1/4 cup cherry tomatoes, halved
    5. **Dressing**: 2 tablespoons lemon juice, 1 tablespoon olive oil, 1 teaspoon Dijon mustard, salt and pepper
- **Instructions**:
    1. In a bowl, combine the mixed greens, cucumber, and cherry tomatoes.
    2. Add the cooked shrimp on top.
    3. In a small bowl, whisk together the dressing ingredients and drizzle over the salad.
- **Nutritional Benefits**: This light salad is low in calories but high in protein from the shrimp, making it perfect for a light lunch or dinner.

Chapter 8: Creative Flavor Combinations and Unexpected Ingredients

Salads are versatile, and one of the best things about making them is the ability to experiment with new and exciting flavor combinations. Whether you're mixing fruits and savory ingredients, adding a bit of spice, or using unexpected ingredients to create something completely new, this chapter will inspire you to think outside the box and create salads that are anything but ordinary.

1. Fruits in Salads: The Sweet and Savory Mix

One of the best ways to add a unique twist to your salad is by combining fruits with savory ingredients. The natural sweetness of fruits can balance out bitter greens, creamy cheeses, and tangy dressings, creating a harmonious mix of flavors.

Strawberry and Goat Cheese Salad

- **Prep Time**: 10 minutes
- **Ingredients**:

1. 2 cups mixed greens (spinach, arugula, or lettuce)
2. 1 cup strawberries, sliced
3. 1/4 cup goat cheese, crumbled
4. 1/4 cup candied pecans
5. **Dressing**: 2 tablespoons balsamic vinegar, 1 tablespoon olive oil, 1 teaspoon honey, salt and pepper to taste

- **Instructions**:
  1. Combine the greens, sliced strawberries, goat cheese, and candied pecans in a bowl.
  2. In a small bowl, whisk together the dressing ingredients.
  3. Drizzle the dressing over the salad and toss gently.
- **Nutritional Benefits**: Strawberries add vitamin C, and goat cheese offers a creamy contrast. The pecans provide healthy fats, and balsamic vinegar adds a tangy sweetness.

Peach and Burrata Salad

- **Prep Time**: 10 minutes
- **Ingredients**:
    1. 2 peaches, sliced
    2. 1 ball burrata cheese
    3. 2 cups arugula or mixed greens
    4. 1/4 cup pistachios, chopped
    5. **Dressing**: 1 tablespoon honey, 2 tablespoons olive oil, 1 tablespoon lemon juice, salt and pepper
- **Instructions**:
    1. Arrange the peaches and burrata on a platter.
    2. Layer with arugula or mixed greens and top with chopped pistachios.
    3. Drizzle with the honey, olive oil, and lemon dressing, and season with salt and pepper.
- **Nutritional Benefits**: Peaches provide vitamin C and antioxidants, while burrata adds protein and creaminess. Pistachios give a satisfying crunch and healthy fats.

2. Spicy and Savory: Adding a Kick

If you love a little heat, adding spicy ingredients to your salad can make it exciting and bold. From chili peppers to spicy dressings, here are some ways to spice up your salad.

Spicy Mango and Avocado Salad

- **Prep Time**: 10 minutes
- **Ingredients**:
    1. 1 mango, diced
    2. 1 avocado, diced
    3. 1/4 cup red onion, thinly sliced
    4. 1 small jalapeño, finely chopped
    5. 1 tablespoon cilantro, chopped
    6. **Dressing**: 1 tablespoon lime juice, 2 tablespoons olive oil, 1 teaspoon honey, salt and pepper to taste
- **Instructions**:
    1. In a bowl, combine the mango, avocado, red onion, jalapeño, and cilantro.
    2. In a small bowl, whisk together the lime juice, olive oil, honey, salt, and pepper.

3. Drizzle the dressing over the salad and toss gently.

- **Nutritional Benefits**: Mango provides vitamin C, while avocado offers healthy fats. Jalapeños give a spicy kick and boost metabolism, while cilantro adds freshness.

Sriracha and Lime Shrimp Salad

- **Prep Time**: 10 minutes
- **Cook Time**: 5 minutes
- **Ingredients**:
    1. 1/2 pound shrimp, peeled and deveined
    2. 1 tablespoon sriracha sauce
    3. 1 tablespoon lime juice
    4. 2 cups mixed greens
    5. 1/4 cup cucumber, sliced
    6. 1/4 cup red cabbage, shredded
    7. **Dressing**: 2 tablespoons olive oil, 1 tablespoon rice vinegar, 1 teaspoon soy sauce, 1 teaspoon honey

- **Instructions**:
    1. Toss the shrimp with sriracha sauce and lime juice. Grill or pan-fry the shrimp for 2-3 minutes per side until cooked.
    2. In a bowl, combine the mixed greens, cucumber, and red cabbage.
    3. In a small bowl, whisk together the dressing ingredients and drizzle over the salad.
    4. Top the salad with the cooked shrimp and serve.
- **Nutritional Benefits**: Shrimp is a great source of lean protein, while the sriracha adds a spicy punch. The cabbage and cucumber provide fiber, and olive oil offers healthy fats.

3. Nuts and Seeds: Crunch and Nutrition

Adding nuts and seeds to your salads not only enhances texture but also boosts their nutritional value. These ingredients provide protein, healthy fats, and a satisfying crunch.

Apple and Walnut Salad

- **Prep Time**: 5 minutes

- **Ingredients**:

    1. 1 apple, sliced
    2. 2 cups arugula
    3. 1/4 cup walnuts, toasted
    4. 1/4 cup blue cheese, crumbled
    5. **Dressing**: 2 tablespoons balsamic vinegar, 1 tablespoon olive oil, 1 teaspoon maple syrup, salt and pepper

- **Instructions**:

    1. In a bowl, combine arugula, apple slices, walnuts, and blue cheese.
    2. In a small bowl, whisk together balsamic vinegar, olive oil, maple syrup, salt, and pepper.
    3. Drizzle the dressing over the salad and toss gently.

- **Nutritional Benefits**: Apples provide fiber, while walnuts offer healthy fats and protein. Blue cheese adds a creamy, tangy flavor.

Roasted Pumpkin Seed and Avocado Salad

- **Prep Time**: 10 minutes
- **Ingredients**:
    1. 1 avocado, diced
    2. 2 cups mixed greens (spinach, kale, arugula)
    3. 1/4 cup roasted pumpkin seeds
    4. 1/4 cup cherry tomatoes, halved
    5. **Dressing**: 2 tablespoons olive oil, 1 tablespoon lime juice, 1 teaspoon cumin, salt and pepper to taste
- **Instructions**:
    1. Combine the mixed greens, avocado, cherry tomatoes, and pumpkin seeds in a bowl.
    2. In a small bowl, whisk together the olive oil, lime juice, cumin, salt, and pepper.
    3. Drizzle the dressing over the salad and toss gently.
- **Nutritional Benefits**: Avocado provides healthy fats, pumpkin seeds offer protein and zinc, and the greens are rich in vitamins A and K.

4. Cheese and Protein: Balancing Flavor and Texture

Adding cheese or protein to your salad can make it more filling and elevate the overall flavor profile. Whether it's a creamy cheese like burrata or a more robust flavor like Parmesan, cheese can take a salad to the next level.

Parmesan and Roasted Cauliflower Salad

- **Prep Time**: 10 minutes
- **Cook Time**: 25 minutes
- **Ingredients**:
    1. 1 head cauliflower, cut into florets
    2. 2 tablespoons olive oil
    3. 1/4 cup grated Parmesan cheese
    4. 2 cups mixed greens
    5. **Dressing**: 2 tablespoons lemon juice, 2 tablespoons olive oil, salt and pepper
- **Instructions**:
    1. Preheat the oven to 400°F (200°C). Toss the cauliflower florets with olive oil, salt, and pepper, and roast for 25 minutes.

2. In a bowl, combine the roasted cauliflower and mixed greens.
3. Drizzle with lemon-olive oil dressing and top with grated Parmesan cheese.

- **Nutritional Benefits**: Cauliflower is rich in fiber and vitamin C, while Parmesan adds a savory umami flavor and calcium.

Bacon and Spinach Salad

- **Prep Time**: 10 minutes
- **Cook Time**: 10 minutes
- **Ingredients**:
    1. 4 slices bacon, cooked and crumbled
    2. 2 cups spinach
    3. 1/4 cup red onion, thinly sliced
    4. 1/4 cup boiled eggs, chopped
    5. **Dressing**: 3 tablespoons olive oil, 1 tablespoon apple cider vinegar, 1 teaspoon mustard, salt and pepper to taste

- **Instructions**:

    1. Combine the spinach, bacon, red onion, and chopped eggs in a bowl.

    2. In a small bowl, whisk together the dressing ingredients and pour over the salad. Toss and serve.

- **InNutritional Benefits**: Bacon provides protein and flavor, while spinach offers fiber and vitamins. Eggs add additional protein and healthy fats.

Chapter 9: Salads for Every Occasion: Impressing Guests and Gathering-Friendly Recipes

Salads are not only a great meal on their own but can also be the star of any gathering or special occasion. Whether you're hosting a dinner party, bringing a dish to a potluck, or just want to make your family dinner more exciting, salads can be elevated to match the occasion. In this chapter, we'll explore how to create salads that fit a variety of events, from casual get-togethers to elegant dinner parties. These recipes are designed to impress your guests while still being easy to prepare.

1. Party-Perfect Pasta Salad

Pasta salad is a versatile and crowd-pleasing option that can be made ahead of time, leaving you more time to enjoy the party. The key is to use ingredients that are fresh, vibrant, and full of flavor.

Mediterranean Pasta Salad

- **Prep Time**: 15 minutes
- **Cook Time**: 10 minutes

- **Ingredients**:
    1. 2 cups cooked pasta (penne or rotini)
    2. 1 cup cherry tomatoes, halved
    3. 1/2 cucumber, diced
    4. 1/4 cup Kalamata olives, sliced
    5. 1/4 cup red onion, thinly sliced
    6. 1/4 cup feta cheese, crumbled
    7. **Dressing**: 3 tablespoons olive oil, 1 tablespoon red wine vinegar, 1 teaspoon Dijon mustard, 1 teaspoon dried oregano, salt and pepper to taste
- **Instructions**:
    1. Cook the pasta according to the package instructions. Drain and let it cool.
    2. In a large bowl, combine the pasta with cherry tomatoes, cucumber, olives, red onion, and feta.
    3. In a small bowl, whisk together the dressing ingredients.
    4. Pour the dressing over the salad and toss gently. Chill in the fridge for at least 30 minutes before serving.

- **Nutritional Benefits**: This salad is packed with vegetables, providing fiber and vitamins, and feta cheese adds a creamy, savory flavor. The olive oil offers heart-healthy fats.

2. Elegant Dinner Party Salads

For dinner parties or more formal gatherings, salads should be elegant and refined, using high-quality ingredients that elevate the dining experience. These salads often feature seasonal produce, fresh herbs, and premium cheeses.

Pear and Blue Cheese Salad with Walnuts

- **Prep Time**: 10 minutes
- **Ingredients**:
    1. 2 pears, sliced
    2. 2 cups mixed greens (arugula, spinach)
    3. 1/4 cup crumbled blue cheese
    4. 1/4 cup toasted walnuts
    5. 1/4 cup pomegranate seeds
    6. **Dressing**: 2 tablespoons olive oil, 1 tablespoon honey, 1 tablespoon balsamic

vinegar, salt and pepper to taste

- **Instructions**:

    1. In a large bowl, combine the mixed greens, pear slices, and pomegranate seeds.
    2. Top with crumbled blue cheese and toasted walnuts.
    3. In a small bowl, whisk together the honey, olive oil, balsamic vinegar, salt, and pepper.
    4. Drizzle the dressing over the salad and toss gently.

- **Nutritional Benefits**: Pears add fiber and vitamin C, while blue cheese provides protein and calcium. Walnuts offer healthy fats, and pomegranate seeds add antioxidants.

3. Summer BBQ Salads

A BBQ is all about comfort food, but you can still add a refreshing, colorful salad to the spread. These salads are easy to make and pair perfectly with grilled meats and sides.

Corn, Avocado, and Tomato Salad

- **Prep Time**: 10 minutes
- **Ingredients**:
    1. 2 cups corn kernels (fresh or frozen)
    2. 1 avocado, diced
    3. 1 cup cherry tomatoes, halved
    4. 1/4 red onion, thinly sliced
    5. 1 tablespoon cilantro, chopped
    6. **Dressing**: 2 tablespoons olive oil, 1 tablespoon lime juice, salt and pepper to taste
- **Instructions**:
    1. If using fresh corn, grill or boil it until tender, then remove the kernels.
    2. In a bowl, combine the corn, avocado, cherry tomatoes, red onion, and cilantro.
    3. Drizzle with olive oil and lime juice, and toss gently. Season with salt and pepper.
- **Nutritional Benefits**: Avocados provide healthy fats, while corn adds fiber and energy-boosting carbohydrates. Tomatoes are rich in antioxidants like lycopene.

4. Holiday Feast Salads

During the holiday season, salads should feel festive, with ingredients that celebrate the season's bounty. Add rich, earthy flavors like roasted vegetables, cranberries, and nuts for a beautiful and seasonal salad.

Roasted Brussels Sprout and Cranberry Salad

- **Prep Time**: 10 minutes
- **Cook Time**: 20 minutes
- **Ingredients**:
    1. 2 cups Brussels sprouts, halved and roasted
    2. 1/2 cup dried cranberries
    3. 1/4 cup pecans, toasted
    4. 2 cups mixed greens (baby kale or spinach)
    5. **Dressing**: 2 tablespoons olive oil, 1 tablespoon maple syrup, 1 tablespoon apple cider vinegar, salt and pepper to taste
- **Instructions**:

1. Preheat the oven to 400°F (200°C). Toss the Brussels sprouts with olive oil, salt, and pepper, and roast for 20 minutes until golden and tender.

2. In a bowl, combine the roasted Brussels sprouts, cranberries, pecans, and mixed greens.

3. In a small bowl, whisk together the maple syrup, apple cider vinegar, olive oil, salt, and pepper.

4. Drizzle the dressing over the salad and toss gently.

- **Nutritional Benefits**: Brussels sprouts are rich in vitamins K and C, while cranberries add antioxidants. Pecans provide healthy fats and add crunch.

5. Potluck Salads

For potlucks and gatherings, you'll want a salad that can be easily transported and enjoyed by a crowd. These salads should be simple to make in large batches and flavorful enough to stand out among other dishes.

Classic Caesar Salad

- **Prep Time**: 10 minutes

- **Ingredients**:
    1. 4 cups Romaine lettuce, chopped
    2. 1/4 cup grated Parmesan cheese
    3. 1 cup croutons
    4. **Dressing**: 3 tablespoons olive oil, 1 tablespoon Dijon mustard, 2 tablespoons lemon juice, 2 tablespoons Worcestershire sauce, 1 clove garlic, minced, salt and pepper to taste
- **Instructions**:
    1. In a large bowl, combine the chopped Romaine lettuce, grated Parmesan, and croutons.
    2. In a small bowl, whisk together the dressing ingredients.
    3. Pour the dressing over the salad and toss to combine.
- **Nutritional Benefits**: Romaine lettuce provides fiber, while Parmesan cheese offers protein and calcium. The dressing is tangy and rich, bringing everything together.

6. Brunch Salads

Brunch is a time to indulge, and salads for this occasion should be light yet satisfying, pairing well with eggs, fresh fruit, and other brunch favorites.

Smoked Salmon and Avocado Salad

- **Prep Time**: 5 minutes
- **Ingredients**:
    1. 2 cups mixed greens (arugula, spinach, and baby kale)
    2. 1 avocado, sliced
    3. 4 ounces smoked salmon
    4. 1/4 red onion, thinly sliced
    5. 1 tablespoon capers
    6. **Dressing**: 1 tablespoon olive oil, 1 tablespoon lemon juice, 1 teaspoon Dijon mustard, salt and pepper to taste
- **Instructions**:
    1. Combine the mixed greens, avocado slices, smoked salmon, red onion, and capers in a bowl.
    2. Whisk together the olive oil, lemon juice, Dijon mustard, salt, and pepper in a small bowl.

3. Drizzle the dressing over the salad and toss gently.

- **Nutritional Benefits**: This salad is packed with protein from the smoked salmon, healthy fats from avocado, and fiber from the greens.

7. Baby Shower or Bridal Shower Salad

For light and celebratory events like baby showers or bridal showers, salads should be refreshing, bright, and easy to eat in a social setting.

Citrus and Almond Salad

- **Prep Time**: 10 minutes
- **Ingredients**:
    1. 2 cups mixed greens (baby spinach, arugula)
    2. 1 orange, peeled and segmented
    3. 1/2 grapefruit, peeled and segmented
    4. 1/4 cup sliced almonds, toasted
    5. **Dressing**: 2 tablespoons olive oil, 1 tablespoon orange juice, 1 teaspoon honey, salt and pepper to taste

- **Instructions**:

    1. Combine the mixed greens, orange segments, and grapefruit segments in a bowl.

    2. Top with toasted almonds.

    3. Whisk together the dressing ingredients and drizzle over the salad. Toss gently.

- **Nutritional Benefits**: Citrus fruits are high in vitamin C and antioxidants, while almonds provide healthy fats and crunch.

Chapter 10: Storing, Packing, and Transporting Salads for Convenience

Whether you're meal prepping for the week, packing a lunch for work, or taking a dish to a picnic, knowing how to store, pack, and transport your salads properly is essential to keeping them fresh, flavorful, and enjoyable. This chapter will guide you through the best practices for storing salads, packing them for lunch, and transporting them to events or gatherings, ensuring your salads stay as fresh as when you made them.

1. How to Store Salad Ingredients for Maximum Freshness

Proper storage is key to keeping your salad ingredients fresh for as long as possible. Here are some tips for storing various salad components:

Storing Greens

- **Best Method**: Keep leafy greens like spinach, lettuce, and kale in a clean, dry container. For extra freshness, line the container with a paper towel to absorb excess moisture.

- **Tip**: Store greens in the crisper drawer of your fridge, as it maintains a consistent, cool temperature. Avoid washing greens until you're ready to use them, as excess moisture can lead to wilting.

Storing Grains and Proteins

- **Best Method**: Cooked grains (like quinoa, rice, or farro) and proteins (such as grilled chicken, tofu, or beans) should be stored in airtight containers in the fridge.
- **Tip**: Allow grains and proteins to cool to room temperature before storing to prevent condensation and sogginess.

Storing Fruits

- **Best Method**: Fruits like berries, apples, and oranges should be stored in separate containers to avoid squashing. For fruits like berries that spoil quickly, place a paper towel at the bottom of the container to absorb moisture.
- **Tip**: Store fruits like apples and pears in the crisper drawer or a fruit basket on the countertop. Keep delicate fruits like strawberries in a breathable container to prevent mold.

Storing Dressings

- **Best Method**: Homemade dressings can be stored in mason jars or airtight containers in the fridge for up to one week. Vinaigrettes last longer than creamy dressings.

- **Tip**: Always store dressings separately from salads until you're ready to serve. If the dressing separates over time, give it a good shake before using.

2. How to Pack Salads for Lunch or a Meal on the Go

Packing salads for lunch or a meal on the go requires a bit of planning to ensure they stay fresh and don't get soggy. Here are some practical tips to make sure your salad stays intact:

Layering Your Salad for Freshness

- **Wet Ingredients on the Bottom**: If you're using a jar or container, start by placing your dressing at the bottom. This keeps the greens from absorbing the liquid and becoming soggy.

- **Hearty Ingredients in the Middle**: Add grains, proteins, and other heavier ingredients (like beans or roasted vegetables) in the middle layers of the container.

- **Greens on Top**: Finally, layer your fresh greens at the top of the container to prevent them from coming into contact with the dressing.

- **Packing Dressings Separately**: Always pack your dressing in a separate container or small jar. You can also use a small dressing container with a leak-proof lid.

Using Mason Jars for Packing

- **Why Mason Jars?** Mason jars are an excellent option for packing salads. Their airtight seal helps keep the ingredients fresh, and their tall shape allows for layering.

- **How to Layer**:

    1. Place the dressing at the bottom of the jar.

    2. Add sturdy vegetables (like carrots, cucumbers, or bell peppers) next.

    3. Add grains or proteins.

    4. Add any soft vegetables or fruits.

    5. Top with leafy greens.

    6. Seal the jar and refrigerate.

- **Tip**: When ready to eat, shake the jar vigorously to distribute the dressing, or dump the salad into a bowl and toss.

3. Transporting Salads to Picnics, Potlucks, or Gatherings

When you're taking your salad to a picnic, potluck, or gathering, it's important to pack it in a way that ensures it stays fresh and doesn't get damaged during transport.

Choose the Right Container

- **Leak-Proof Containers**: For transporting salads, look for leak-proof, airtight containers. This will prevent any dressing from spilling and keep the ingredients secure.

- **Use a Cooler for Temperature-Sensitive Ingredients**: If your salad contains perishable items (like dairy or meat), make sure to pack it in a cooler with ice packs to keep it cold.

- **Opt for Shallow Containers**: A shallow container will allow the ingredients to stay evenly distributed and reduce the chance of things shifting or getting squished.

Packing for a Picnic or Potluck

- **Dressing on the Side**: Always pack your dressing separately. If you're serving a salad with multiple people, bring the dressing in a separate bottle or jar so people can add as much or as little as they like.

- **Keep It Simple for Transport**: If you're bringing a large salad to a potluck or picnic, consider keeping it simple and opting for ingredients that won't get damaged during transport, like beans, grains, or roasted vegetables.

- **Consider Using Cling Film or Foil**: If you're worried about salad ingredients shifting around, you can use plastic wrap or aluminum foil to cover the top of the salad in the container for extra stability.

4. How to Keep Salad Fresh for Longer

Sometimes, you may need to store a salad for longer than a day or pack it ahead of time. Here's how to keep your salad as fresh as possible:

Use an Airtight Container

An airtight container helps preserve the freshness of the salad and prevents wilting. It also reduces exposure to air, which can cause salads to dry out.

Avoid Storing Wet Ingredients Together

If you plan to store your salad for a few days, separate any wet ingredients like cucumbers, tomatoes, or fruits. These ingredients can release moisture and cause the salad to become soggy.

Use Paper Towels

For leafy greens, placing a paper towel in the container with the salad helps absorb excess moisture, keeping your greens crisper for longer.

Refrigeration

Store salads in the refrigerator as soon as possible, especially if they contain perishable ingredients. Salads should be eaten within 3-4 days to ensure the best flavor and texture.

5. Making Salads Ahead of Time for Busy Weeks

If you want to make salads for the entire week in one go, the key is to prep the ingredients, but keep them in separate containers so that they remain fresh.

Prep Ingredients in Bulk

- Wash and chop your veggies, fruits, and greens.
- Cook any grains or proteins, then store them separately in airtight containers.

Build Salad Kits

You can build salad kits for the week by packing each meal in its own container. When you're ready to eat, just toss the salad together with dressing. This method saves time and keeps everything fresh.

Freezing Salad Components

For even longer storage, you can freeze certain salad components, like cooked grains or roasted vegetables. Just make sure to store them in airtight freezer bags or containers and label them with the date.

Chapter 11: Final Thoughts: Making Salads a Fun and Easy Part of Your Routine

Salads don't have to be complicated to be delicious and satisfying. With the right ingredients, a little creativity, and a few simple techniques, salads can become a regular part of your meals, bringing a wealth of nutrients, flavor, and variety to your diet. In this final chapter, we'll discuss some tips for incorporating salads into your daily routine, making them more enjoyable, and helping you stay motivated to eat fresh, healthy meals.

1. Incorporating More Salads Into Your Diet

If you're looking to eat more salads but aren't sure where to start, the key is to make it as easy and enjoyable as possible. Here are some strategies for adding more salads to your routine:

Start Small and Build Up

If you're not used to eating salads every day, start with simple, small salads and gradually work your way up to more elaborate ones. Begin with a side salad with dinner or a light lunch salad, and then experiment with more complex combinations as you get more comfortable.

Use Salads as a Meal Base

Salads can be the perfect base for a meal. Start with greens or grains as your foundation and add protein (chicken, tofu, beans), veggies, healthy fats (avocado, nuts, seeds), and a dressing of your choice. This approach ensures that your salad is both filling and satisfying, providing a full range of nutrients.

Make Salads a Snack

Salads don't always have to be a full meal. You can enjoy a smaller, lighter salad as a snack. Opt for a fresh veggie salad with a simple vinaigrette or a fruit salad to curb your hunger in between meals.

Swap Processed Foods for Salads

Try swapping out processed foods like chips, crackers, or even sandwiches with a hearty salad. By doing this, you're replacing calorie-dense, nutrient-poor foods with fiber-rich, nutrient-dense greens and veggies, which will leave you feeling fuller longer and support overall health.

2. Making Salad Prep a Weekly Routine

One of the biggest barriers to eating salads regularly is the time it takes to prepare fresh ingredients. The good news is that meal prepping salads can be a quick and easy task that saves time throughout the week. Here's how to make salad prep a part of your weekly routine:

Set Aside Time for Prep

Dedicate an hour or so each week to wash, chop, and prep your salad ingredients. This can include washing greens, chopping veggies, cooking grains or proteins, and storing everything in airtight containers. When everything is ready to go, you can assemble a salad in minutes.

Create Salad Kits

Create "salad kits" by pre-portioning your ingredients into separate containers or mason jars. For example, you can store greens in one container, proteins in another, and dressings in small jars. This will allow you to quickly assemble a salad without any prep work on busy days.

Store Ingredients Properly

As mentioned in previous chapters, storing your ingredients properly ensures freshness and longevity. By keeping salad components in airtight containers and keeping dressings separate, you can extend the shelf life of your salad ingredients, which helps reduce food waste and makes it easier to grab a healthy meal at any time.

3. Making Salads Exciting: Experiment with New Ingredients

Eating the same salad every day can get boring, so don't be afraid to experiment with new ingredients, textures, and flavors. Here are some ways to spice up your salad routine:

Try Different Greens

While lettuce and spinach are great staples, don't be afraid to mix it up with different leafy greens like arugula, kale, watercress, or mustard greens. These greens bring a variety of textures and flavors to your salads.

Incorporate Seasonal Ingredients

As we discussed in the seasonal salads chapter, using seasonal ingredients will ensure your salads are always fresh and in tune with the flavors of the time of year. Summer brings tomatoes, cucumbers, and berries, while fall offers roasted squashes, Brussels sprouts, and pomegranates. Embrace the seasons and the variety they bring.

Add New Proteins

While grilled chicken and tofu are great salad toppers, try branching out and adding proteins like grilled shrimp, boiled eggs, roasted chickpeas, or even leftover steak. The variety will add new flavors and keep things interesting.

Play with Toppings

Toppings are an easy way to add variety to your salad. Consider adding different types of seeds, nuts, cheese, or even roasted vegetables. For something fun, try crispy fried shallots, pickled onions, or a drizzle of balsamic glaze.

4. Salads for Health Goals

Salads can be tailored to meet your specific health goals, whether you're focusing on weight loss, muscle building, or overall wellness. Here are a few ways to adjust your salad ingredients to fit your needs:

For Weight Loss

To create a salad that helps with weight loss, focus on ingredients that are low in calories but high in nutrients and fiber. Load your salad with leafy greens, non-starchy vegetables (like cucumbers, tomatoes, and bell peppers), and lean proteins (like chicken breast or tofu). Avoid heavy dressings and opt for lighter vinaigrettes or yogurt-based dressings.

For Muscle Building

If you're looking to build muscle, salads can be packed with protein to help repair and grow muscle tissue. Include lean meats, fish, or plant-based proteins like lentils and chickpeas. Add healthy fats like avocado, nuts, or seeds, and consider including quinoa, farro, or beans for complex carbohydrates to fuel your workouts.

For Detoxing and Digestive Health

For detoxifying salads or improving digestion, focus on ingredients that are rich in fiber, antioxidants, and enzymes. Cruciferous vegetables (like broccoli, cauliflower, and kale), citrus fruits, and high-fiber grains (like quinoa or oats) are all great choices. Include a lemon-based dressing to help cleanse your system, and don't forget to hydrate with plenty of water!

5. Tips for Serving Salads to Guests

Salads can be the perfect addition to any dinner party, potluck, or gathering. Here are some tips for serving salads to guests:

Make It Visually Appealing

When serving salads for a group, presentation matters! Choose a large, attractive bowl or platter and make sure the ingredients are evenly distributed. Garnish the salad with fresh herbs, edible flowers, or colorful ingredients like pomegranate seeds, slices of citrus, or nuts to add a pop of color.

Serve Dressing on the Side

Not everyone likes the same amount of dressing, so it's a good idea to serve the dressing on the side. This way, guests can add as much or as little as they want.

Consider Dietary Restrictions

When serving salads to a group, it's important to accommodate dietary preferences and restrictions. Make sure to offer a variety of options—like a vegan salad, gluten-free options, or a salad with a dairy-free dressing—so everyone can enjoy.

Serve as a Main or Side

Salads can be a main course or a side dish. If you're serving it as a main, make sure it's hearty enough with